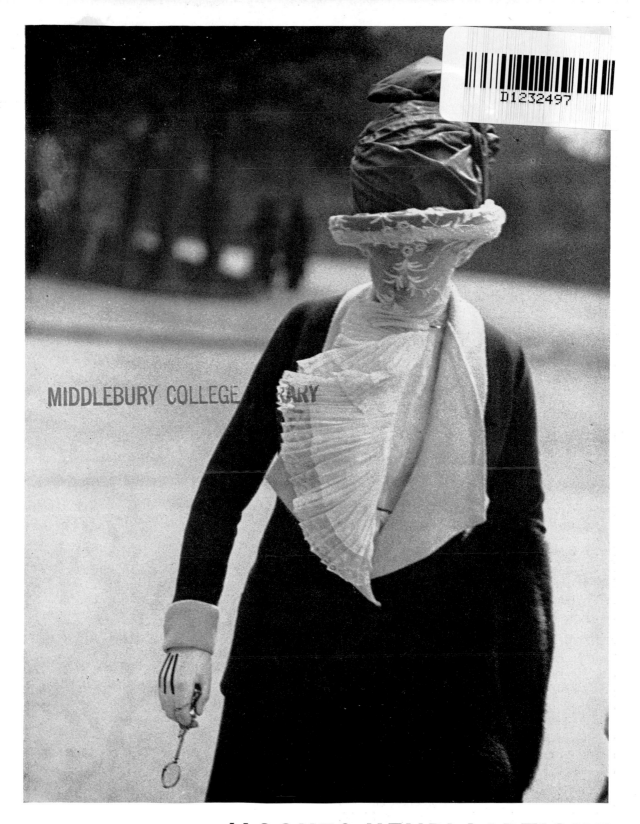

the photographs of **JACQUES HENRI LARTIGUE**

the museum of modern art, new york

ACKNOWLEDGMENTS

The Museum gratefully acknowledges its indebtedness to Jacques Henri Lartigue for his generous gift to the Museum Collections of most of the photographs reproduced in this publication, and to Charles Rado of Rapho-Guillumette, who first brought the pictures to the Museum's attention, and who cooperated in the gathering of documentary information.

Forty-two photographs by Lartigue were shown in the photography section of the Museum Collections galleries during the summer of 1963.

The Museum of Modern Art Bulletin, Volume XXX, No. 1, 1963.
Front cover: Avenue des Acacias, 1911.

the photographs of
JACQUES HENRI LARTIGUE

It is easier for an old photograph to be interesting than it is for a new one. To show clearly the life of our own time and place demands acute perception, for our eyes grow accustomed to the everyday miracles. But it would seem that the pictures in an old album need only to have been sharply focused and clearly printed, in order to reveal the sense and spirit of their past time.

Time works in favor of the honest photograph, and will in fifty years often turn a banal record into a moving souvenir, sweet with the slight poetry of nostalgia. But the photography of Jacques Henri Lartigue is a different case: here the persuasive charm of a vanished world may hide the work's deeper beauty. For these pictures are the observations of genius: fresh perceptions, poetically sensed and graphically fixed.

Lartigue was born near Paris in 1896, into an inventive, prosperous, fashionable French family. His father Henri was a banker; his grandfather Alfred (called Delacour) was one of the inventors of the monorail system, and also a dramatist; his brother Maurice designed and built gliders and powered airplanes as early as 1908. Jacques' inventiveness was in his eyes. According to his own recollections, it would seem that he discovered modern photography at the age of five, without a camera:

"During the summer vacations, too young to join in the games of my big brother and his friends —I was their 'spectator' . . . they juggled, did handstands, or held automobile races with crates on wheels.

"I was only a spectator, but secretly, deep inside me, I had made a wonderful discovery! By opening and shutting my eyes in a 'certain fashion' I had found the way of capturing all the images that pleased me! Sometimes when I was in the process of adding a new image to my precious collection, my brother would look at me, and suddenly ask what ailed me, that I stood there bolt upright, like an imbecile.

"It was a superhuman invention! I caught it all! the colors! the sounds, the true measure of things! . . ."

The following year Lartigue made his first photographs, standing on a stool to see the ground-glass of the large tripod camera. But the subject had to be motionless while the lens was uncapped. ". . . Then how could one retain our bicycle races? our jumping contests; our little boat races on the river, and all the inventions that surged before our eyes every day?" The following Christmas, Lartigue received a new hand camera with rapid lens and shutter. This was the "trap of images" that he had known he needed.

Before he was ten years old, Lartigue was making pictures which today seem an astonishing anticipation of the best small-camera work done a generation later.

It is impossible to believe that the visual char-

J. H. Lartigue with his Mother and Grandmother. Bois de Boulogne, Paris, 1905 (Photograph by Henri Lartigue)

acter of the child's work—with its remarkable directness and economy—could be the product of a conscious concern with formal values. It is more likely that work as confidently radical as this could have been achieved only by a true primitive: one working without a sense of obligation either to tradition, or to the known characteristics of his medium. Perhaps only a greatly talented child, left to his own devices, could have made these pictures a half-century ago.

Such an artist needs neither tradition nor training, but he does need great motivation and great talent. The child Lartigue was motivated by an intense love for the world around him. He loved beautiful women, elegant costumes, automobiles, flying machines, speed and games. When even younger he preferred drawing pastels of an imaginary desert (including a lion, a palm tree, and the sun); but soon he became more interested in the "pretty women, eccentric and very elegant . . . in horse drawn carriages or beautiful shining automobiles. . . . It was these women, a little mysterious, so pretty and a little frightening that I encountered at noon in the Bois de Boulogne."

And with great simplicity, the child loved the physical act of seeing. Lartigue saw, as though for the first time, the transient relationships of life in flux. Earlier photography had seen one thing at a time; the individual facts preceded the relationship. But what Lartigue sought was the ephemeral image itself.

He saw the momentary, never to be repeated images created by the accidents of overlapping shapes, and by shapes interrupted by the picture edge (pp. 7, 9, 10). This is the essence of modern photographic seeing: to see not objects but their projected images.

He sensed the active importance—the energy —of the confining picture edge, and filled his picture area with great boldness (pp. 8, 11, 29).

These visual characteristics of Lartigue's work are not his invention, and are only partly his discovery. They are basic to the discipline of the camera, and are visible with increasing frequency during the nineteenth century. But what had been a random tendency of the camera becomes in Lartigue's work a coherent mode of seeing—a new kind of clarity.

If the graphic quality of Lartigue's work suggests the pictures of Degas, Toulouse-Lautrec, and others, it is perhaps because these artists were sensitive to the new camera image—surely not because the ten-year-old had learned from the painters—or from Japanese prints.

Beyond the purely formal aspects of his seeing, Lartigue found a new kind of subject matter. He recognized the moment when human relationships fleetingly revealed themselves. Lartigue's people are aware of each other, and we feel that we are aware of their thoughts (pp. 12, 16, 28). Perhaps no one took the boy and his machine seriously: among hundreds of his photographs one finds not a single self-conscious pose or calculated posture. The photographer might have been invisible, and as a photographer perhaps he was, for in those days a camera was not commonly a child's plaything.

Often, as with lyric poets, the productive years of a creative photographer are too soon over. The photographer is sustained only by his own appetite for life; the medium is a simple and puritan intermediary. Once the photographer's observation falters, there is small solace in the pure pleasures of craft.

By the time of the World War, Lartigue's principle interest was painting, which he studied at the Académie Julian. After the early 'twenties his photographs seem less intense in observation. Between the wars, Lartigue was widely exhibited as a painter, his most important exhibition taking place in 1939 at the Galerie Charpentier, one month before the recurrence of war. Lartigue today lives and paints in Paris and in Opio, near Grasse.

The vigor and freedom of Lartigue's photographs grew from a commitment not to photography but to life. His understanding of the medium, though intense and certain, was neither broad nor subtle. His was an achievement of love and genius, uncomplicated by aesthetic theory or professional ambition. Work so purely motivated can stop as suddenly and as inexplicably as it began. Of the forty-two photographs in The Museum of Modern Art collection, only three postdate the first World War. But in the decade that preceded his own twentieth year, Lartigue looked into the eyes of a changing world, and what he saw there he recorded with a prophetic freshness of vision.

May 1963   John Szarkowski

Gordon Bennett Cup Race, 1905

The Beach at Trouville, 1905

The Beach at Biarritz, 1907

Simone Roussel on the Beach at Villerville, 1906

The Beach at Villerville, 1908

The Beach at Pourville, 1908

Glider Constructed by Maurice Lartigue, Château de Rouzat, 1909

Bois de Boulogne, Paris, 1911

Maurice Lartigue on his "Bobsleigh," Château de Rouzat, 1909

Avenue du Bois de Boulogne, Paris, 1910

Jean Haguet, Château de Rouzat, 1910

At the Races, Auteuil, 1910

The Race Course at Auteuil, Paris, 1910

Professor Aubert of the Sorbonne, Château de Rouzat, 1911

Avenue des Acacias, 1911

Maurice Lartigue, Château de Rouzat, 1911

At the Races, Nice, 1910

Avenue du Bois de Boulogne, Paris, 1911

Wheeled "Bobsleigh" Invented by Jacques Lartigue, 1911

Avenue des Acacias, Paris, 1912

Mary Lancret, Avenue des Acacias, Paris, 1912

The Race Course at Nice, 1912

Jean Haguet, Château de Rouzat, 1910

Motorcycle, 1912

Grand Prix of The Automobile Club of France, 1912

Henri Lartigue Driving, 1914

Combegrasse, Puy de Dôme, 1922

M. Laroze and Louis Ferrand, Kite by Henri Lartigue, Château de Rouzat, 1911